Kelly Clarkson

ABDO
Publishing Company

Big Buddy BOOKS
Buddy Bios

by Sarah Tieck

VISIT US AT
www.abdopublishing.com

Published by ABDO Publishing Company, PO Box 398166, Minneapolis, Minnesota 55439.

Copyright © 2014 by Abdo Consulting Group, Inc. International copyrights reserved in all countries. No part of this book may be reproduced in any form without written permission from the publisher. Big Buddy Books™ is a trademark and logo of ABDO Publishing Company.

Printed in the United States of America, North Mankato, Minnesota.
102013
012014

 PRINTED ON RECYCLED PAPER

Coordinating Series Editor: Rochelle Baltzer
Contributing Editors: Megan M. Gunderson, Bridget O'Brien, Marcia Zappa
Graphic Design: Maria Hosley
Cover Photograph: *Getty Images*: Jeff Kravitz/FilmMagic.
Interior Photographs/Illustrations: *AP Photo*: Joe Cavaretta (p. 15), Express Newspapers via AP Images (p. 5), Carolyn Kaster (p. 25), Paul Sakuma (p. 15), Reed Saxon (p. 21), John Shearer/Invision (p. 28), Paul Skipper (p. 19); *Getty Images*: Jean-Paul Assenard/WireImage (p. 9), Brian Bedder (p. 23), Vince Bucci (p. 7), Getty Images for NARAS (p. 27), SGranitz/WireImage (p. 17), Kevin Winter/ImageDirect/FOX (p. 13); *Shutterstock*: Juan Camilo Bernal (p. 11).

Library of Congress Cataloging-in-Publication Data

Tieck, Sarah, 1976-
  Kelly Clarkson : original American Idol / Sarah Tieck.
    pages cm. -- (Big buddy biographies)
  ISBN 978-1-62403-196-0
1. Clarkson, Kelly, 1982---Juvenile literature. 2. Singers--United States--Biography--Juvenile literature. I. Title.
  ML3930.C523T54 2014
  782.42164092--dc23
  [B]
                          2013029175

Contents

Did you know...

Millions of people watch *American Idol* and vote for their favorite singers.

Singing Star

Kelly Clarkson is a famous singer. She is also known as the first winner of *American Idol*. Since then, she has released albums and received awards for her music.

To win *American Idol*, Kelly had to beat thousands of other singers!

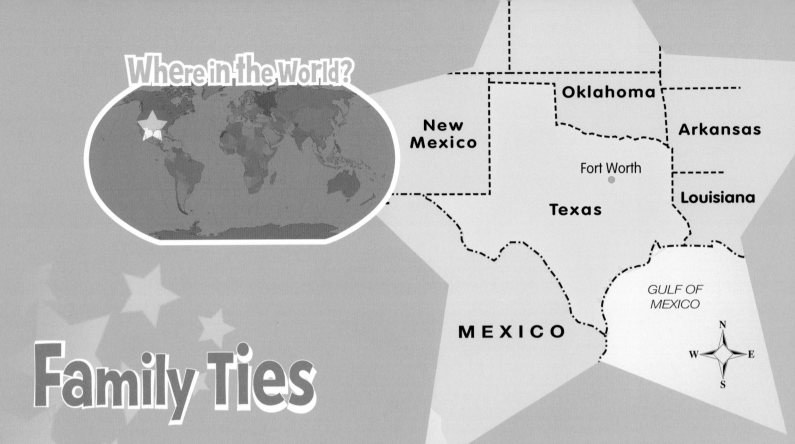

Family Ties

Kelly Brianne Clarkson was born in Fort Worth, Texas, on April 24, 1982. Her parents are Jeanne Rose Taylor and Stephen Clarkson. Her stepfather is Jimmy Taylor. Her brother is Jason and her sister is Alyssa.

When Kelly was six, her parents divorced. Kelly lived with her mother. Jeanne worked hard to care for her family and go to school.

Sometimes, Kelly's mom gets to attend events with her.

Early Years

Kelly enjoyed singing from a young age. Around 1994, a teacher heard Kelly's voice. She got Kelly to join the school's **choir**.

In choir, Kelly improved her singing and became more sure of herself. Around seventh grade, she knew she wanted to be a **professional** singer.

Kelly worked hard to grow her skills as a singer.

Kelly attended Burleson High School. In 2000, she finished high school. Then, she moved to Los Angeles, California.

Kelly had many different jobs there. She wanted a job in the music business. But, she found few opportunities. Then, her apartment was harmed by a fire. So, Kelly decided to move back to Texas.

Many music and entertainment businesses are based in Los Angeles. So, it is a popular city for singers, artists, and actors.

Big Break

In 2002, Kelly heard about **auditions** for *American Idol*. Tryouts for this new talent show were being held in Dallas, Texas. Kelly decided to try out. The judges loved her!

Next, Kelly traveled to Hollywood, California. There, she had more auditions for *American Idol*. She was chosen to be a finalist on the show's first season!

American Idol

American Idol is a popular television show. Each season, young people **compete** to be named the best singer. The show has changed since the first season. There have been many winners and several new judges.

Thousands of people across the country **audition** for the show. Judges choose a small group of finalists to **perform**. Every week, each finalist sings and then viewers vote. Singers with the fewest votes leave the show. Finally, one winner is chosen.

Simon Cowell, Paula Abdul, and Randy Jackson (*left to right*) were the show's original judges. They talked about each performance before viewers voted.

After winning *American Idol*, Kelly went on a concert tour with other *American Idol* singers. She also returned to the show to perform.

Original American Idol

Season one of *American Idol* aired from June until September 2002. During the show, Kelly sang and learned about performing. On the last episode, she sang "A Moment Like This."

When viewers voted, Kelly was the winner! She was given a record contract. After the show, "A Moment Like This" was released as a single. It quickly became number one on the Billboard charts!

At first, Kelly didn't hear that she'd won. She realized it when runner-up Justin Guarini said, "Congratulations."

New Opportunities

After winning *American Idol*, Kelly began recording her first album. She had more opportunities to **perform**. Her dream of becoming a **professional** singer had come true!

In 2003, Kelly's first album was **released**. It is called *Thankful*. It includes pop rock songs, such as "Miss Independent." Kelly's album was a hit. It sold more than 2 million copies!

In 2003, Kelly starred in a movie called *From Justin to Kelly*. Justin Guarini was her costar.

Award Winner

In 2004, Kelly's second album came out. It is called *Breakaway*. It includes songs with a rock sound, such as "Behind These Hazel Eyes," "Breakaway," and "Walk Away."

This album had several hits. And, it earned Kelly two **Grammy Awards**! She was excited to be honored.

In 2006, Kelly won a Grammy Award for *Breakaway*. She also won a Grammy for the song "Since U Been Gone."

21

A Working Singer

After two hit albums, Kelly wanted to keep growing as a singer. In 2007, her third album came out. It is called *My December*.

Kelly helped write songs for this album. She took a stand for her ideas to be included in it.

In 2009, Kelly **released** her fourth album, *All I Ever Wanted*. The first single was "My Life Would Suck Without You." It broke a Billboard chart record by going from number 97 to number 1 in one week!

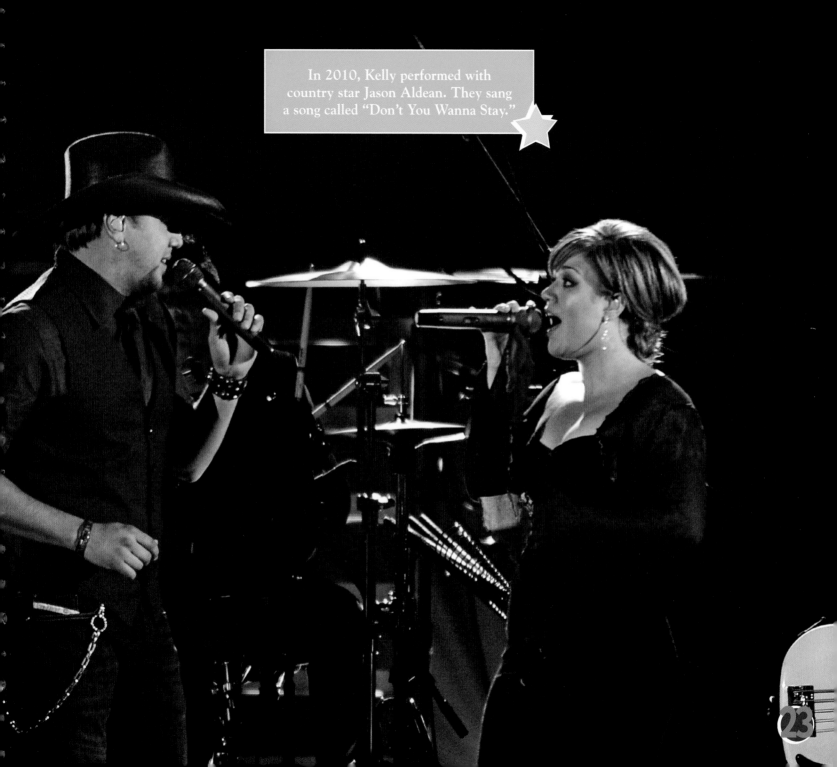

In 2010, Kelly performed with country star Jason Aldean. They sang a song called "Don't You Wanna Stay."

23

A Singer's Life

As a singer and songwriter, Kelly spends time working on her songs. She goes to recording studios to make albums.

After an album comes out, Kelly works hard to **promote** it. She appears on television and in magazines. And, she **performs** live for fans.

In 2013, Kelly sang at the second inauguration of President Barack Obama. She was honored to be part of this important American event.

25

Off the Stage

When Kelly is not working, she spends time at home. In 2012, Brandon Blackstock asked Kelly to marry him. She said yes! They enjoy seeing music together and being active.

Kelly likes to help others. Some groups she helps include March of Dimes and Save the Children.

Kelly and Brandon attend music events together.

At the Grammys in 2013, Kelly was excited to be up against singers such as Adele and Pink!

Buzz

Kelly's fifth album is called *Stronger*. It came out in 2011 and became a hit. In 2013, Kelly won her third **Grammy Award** for this album! Kelly's opportunities keep growing and changing. She continues **performing** her music in concerts and on television. Fans are excited for more music from Kelly Clarkson!

Snapshot

⭐**Name**: Kelly Brianne Clarkson

⭐**Birthday**: April 24, 1982

⭐**Birthplace**: Fort Worth, Texas

⭐**Albums**: *Thankful, Breakaway, My December, All I Ever Wanted, Stronger*

⭐**Appearances**: *American Idol, From Justin to Kelly, Saturday Night Live*

Important Words

air to show on television or play on the radio.

audition (aw-DIH-shuhn) to give a trial performance showcasing personal talent as a musician, a singer, a dancer, or an actor.

choir (KWEYE-uhr) a group of singers that perform together, usually in a church or school.

compete to take part in a contest between two or more persons or groups.

episode one show in a series of shows.

Grammy Award any of the awards given each year by the National Academy of Recording Arts and Sciences. Grammy Awards honor the year's best accomplishments in music.

perform to do something in front of an audience. A performance is the act of doing something, such as singing or acting, in front of an audience.

professional (pruh-FEHSH-nuhl) working for money rather than only for pleasure.

promote to help something become known.

release to make available to the public.

Web Sites

To learn more about Kelly Clarkson, visit ABDO Publishing Company online. Web sites about Kelly Clarkson are featured on our Book Links page. These links are routinely monitored and updated to provide the most current information available.

www.abdopublishing.com

33

Index